MW00897590

Dear Mom, I Want To Know Your Story

Want a freebie?
Email us at

Benzerpress@gmail.com

Title the email «Story!» and we'll send you something fun

What's one of your earliest memories?

_____

_____

_____

_____

_____

When you were my age, what kind of things did you want to do with your life?

_____

_____

_____

_____

_____

What's something you always wanted to do but didn't – and why didn't you?

_____

_____

_____

_____

_____

_____

_____

_____

_____

_____

_____

_____

_____

_____

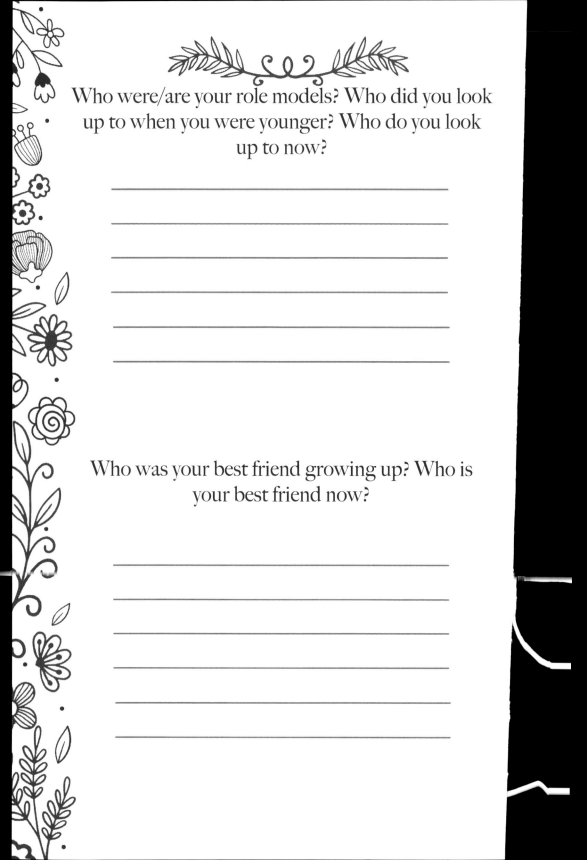

Who were/are your role models? Who did you look up to when you were younger? Who do you look up to now?

_____

_____

_____

_____

_____

Who was your best friend growing up? Who is your best friend now?

_____

_____

_____

_____

_____

How have your notions of what it means to be a
parent changed over your lifetime?

_____

_____

_____

_____

_____

Growing up, what did you think you wanted to do
for a living?

_____

_____

_____

_____

_____

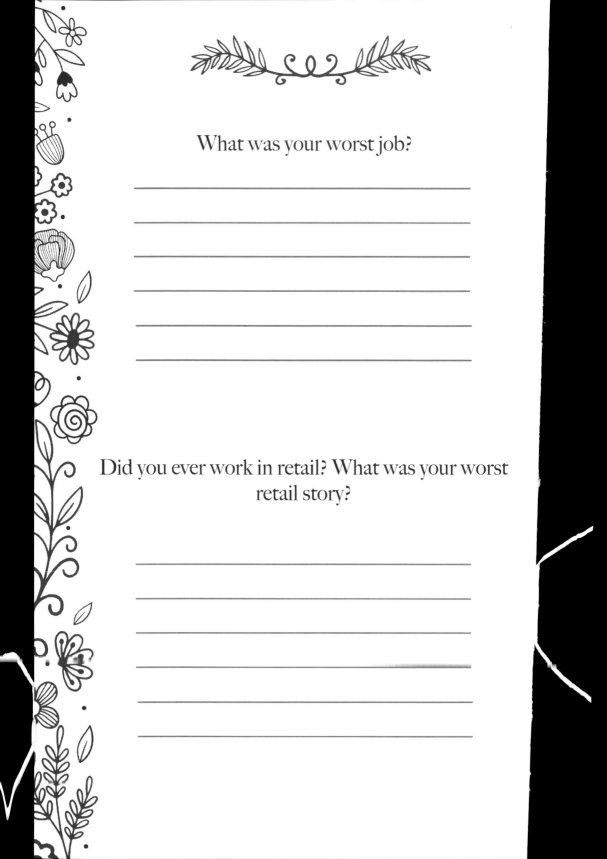

What was your worst job?

_____

_____

_____

_____

_____

Did you ever work in retail? What was your worst retail story?

_____

_____

_____

_____

_____

_____

Did you ever want to start a business? If you could, what business would you own?

_____

_____

_____

_____

_____

What is your dream job?

_____

_____

_____

_____

_____

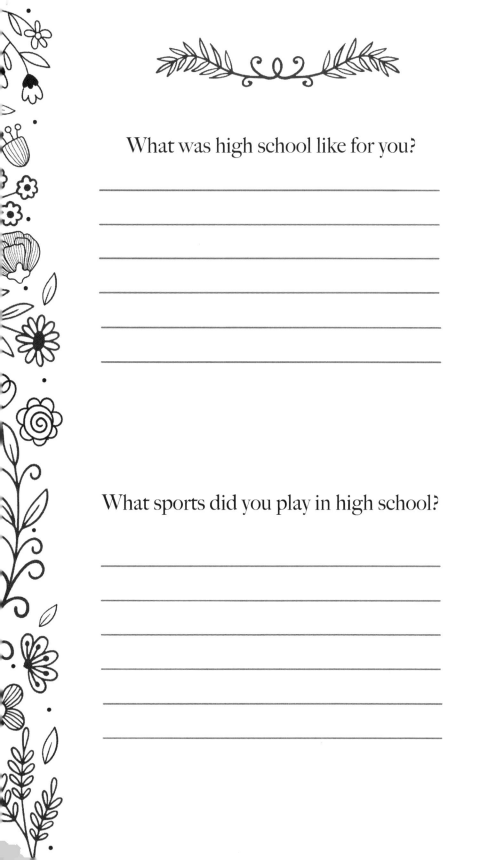

What was high school like for you?

_____
_____
_____
_____
_____

What sports did you play in high school?

_____
_____
_____
_____
_____

How would others describe you in middle school, high school and/or college?

_____

_____

_____

_____

_____

What were some of your biggest struggles or insecurities in high school?

_____

_____

_____

_____

_____

Place a picture and tell its story

_____

_____

_____

_____

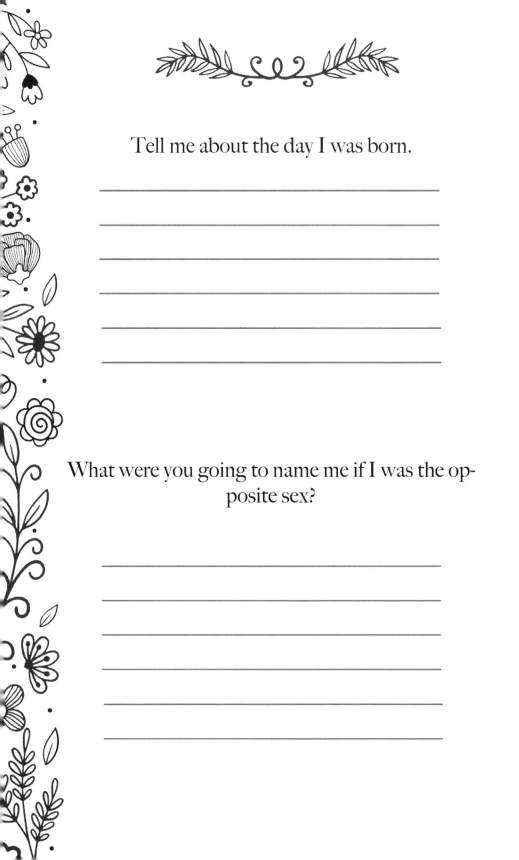

Tell me about the day I was born.

_____

_____

_____

_____

_____

What were you going to name me if I was the opposite sex?

_____

_____

_____

_____

_____

When did you know you were ready to have kids?

_____

_____

_____

_____

_____

What was the moment I frustrated you most when
I was growing up?

_____

_____

_____

_____

_____

What was the moment I hurt you the most when I was growing up?

_____
_____
_____
_____
_____

What was the moment i made happy the most when i was growing up?

_____
_____
_____
_____
_____

How many kids did you originally want to have?

_____

_____

_____

_____

_____

Is there anything that you really want to know
about me?

_____

_____

_____

_____

_____

What was the ex I had that you really couldn't stand?

_____

_____

_____

_____

_____

When you were my age, what kind of things did you want to do with your life?

_____

_____

_____

_____

_____

What do you look for in a friend?

_____

_____

_____

_____

_____

How did you meet your best friend?

_____

_____

_____

_____

_____

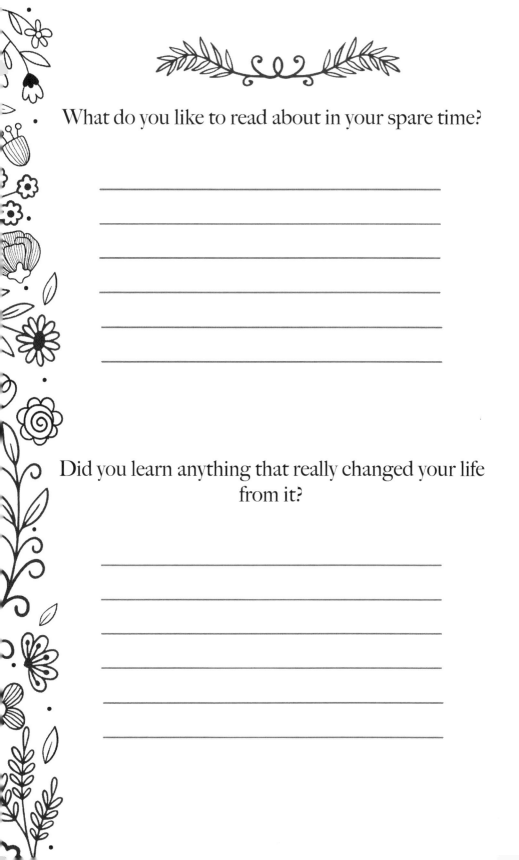

What do you like to read about in your spare time?

_____

_____

_____

_____

_____

Did you learn anything that really changed your life
from it?

_____

_____

_____

_____

_____

What are your most favorite bonding activities to do with me?

_____

_____

_____

_____

_____

Is there any advice you really wish I would take to heart?

_____

_____

_____

_____

_____

Place a picture and tell its story

_____

_____

_____

_____

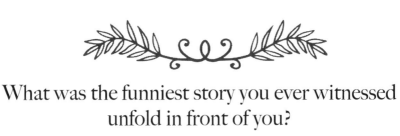

What was the funniest story you ever witnessed
unfold in front of you?

_____

_____

_____

_____

_____

_____

_____

_____

_____

_____

_____

_____

_____

_____

_____

_____

What was the best birthday you've ever had?

_____

_____

_____

_____

_____

What pets did you have when you were young?

_____

_____

_____

_____

_____

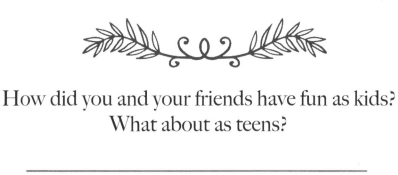

How did you and your friends have fun as kids?
What about as teens?

_____

_____

_____

_____

_____

What were your favorite bands as a teenager?

_____

_____

_____

_____

_____

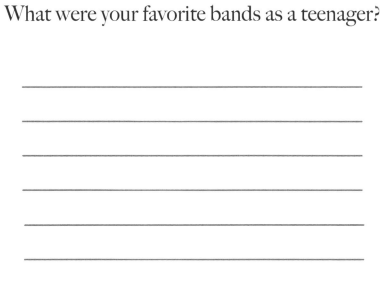

What era would you want to live in, if you could travel through time?

_____

_____

_____

_____

_____

Do you believe in reincarnation? If so, what do you think you did in a past life?

_____

_____

_____

_____

_____

Did you ever see something paranormal in nature? What was it?

_____

_____

_____

_____

_____

Did you ever go to a psychic who predicted something that came true? What was the story?

_____

_____

_____

_____

_____

A genie just decided to give you three wishes.
What would you wish for, and why?

_____

_____

_____

_____

_____

_____

What would you do if you had $100 million?

_____

_____

_____

_____

_____

_____

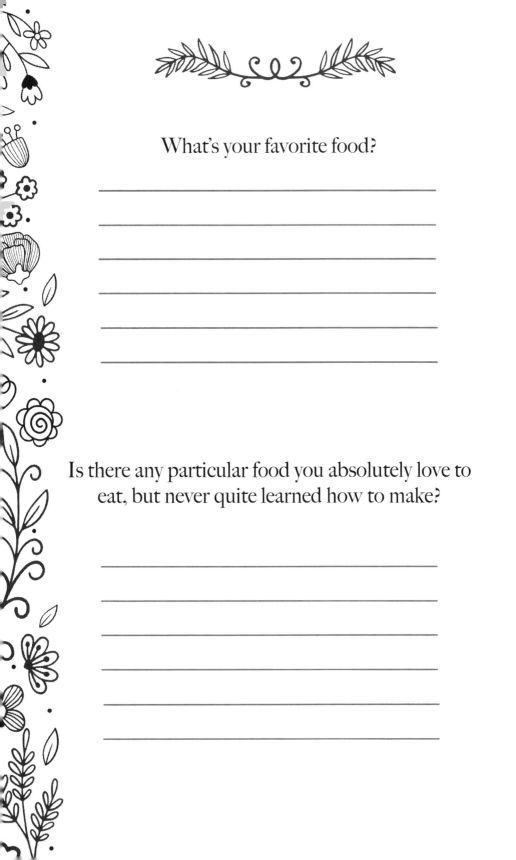

What's your favorite food?

_____

_____

_____

_____

_____

Is there any particular food you absolutely love to eat, but never quite learned how to make?

_____

_____

_____

_____

_____

_____

What's the best trip you've ever taken?

_____

_____

_____

_____

_____

Where would you want to go, for a month-long trip?

_____

_____

_____

_____

_____

Place a picture and tell its story

_____

_____

_____

_____

What was the best vacation you ever went on?

_____

_____

_____

_____

_____

Where have you traveled the furthest?

_____

_____

_____

_____

_____

What are your fears?

_____

_____

_____

_____

_____

_____

What is your most embarrassing moment?

_____

_____

_____

_____

_____

_____

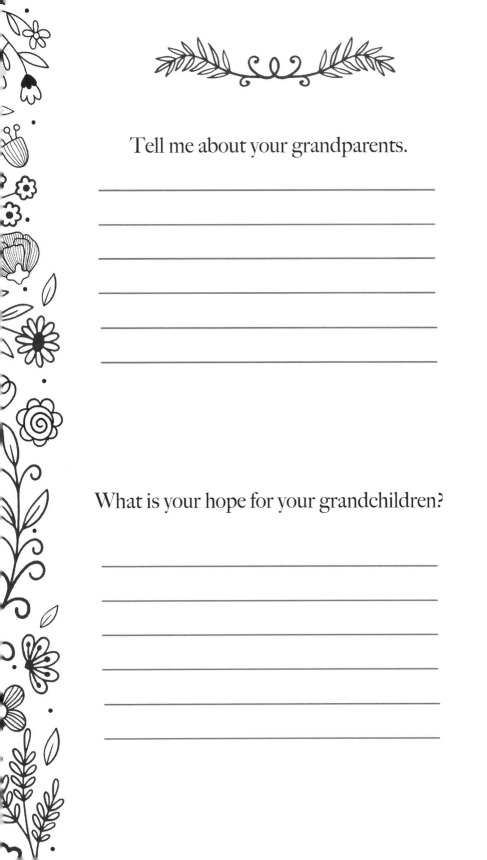

Tell me about your grandparents.

_____

_____

_____

_____

_____

What is your hope for your grandchildren?

_____

_____

_____

_____

_____

What's the hardest thing about raising children?

_____

_____

_____

_____

_____

Is becoming a grandparent different than becoming a parent?

_____

_____

_____

_____

_____

How did you meet Mom/Dad?

_____

_____

_____

_____

_____

When did you know that you were ready to get married?

_____

_____

_____

_____

_____

What was your wedding day like?

_____

_____

_____

_____

_____

What's the worst fight you ever had with my dad/mom?

_____

_____

_____

_____

_____

What was life like for you at my age?

_____

_____

_____

_____

_____

Have you ever done something really impulsive?
How did it go?

_____

_____

_____

_____

_____

Is there a moment or event that radically changed the way you saw the world?

_____

_____

_____

_____

_____

_____

Describe a moment in American history that you will never forget.

_____

_____

_____

_____

_____

_____

Place a picture and tell its story

_____

_____

_____

_____

Do you think money can buy happiness?

_____
_____
_____
_____
_____
_____

How much money does a person need to love life?

_____
_____
_____
_____
_____
_____

If you won the lottery, what would you do with the money?

_____

_____

_____

_____

_____

_____

_____

_____

_____

_____

_____

_____

_____

_____

_____

What's your favorite TV show? Why?

_____

_____

_____

_____

_____

If your life was a reality show, what would it be called?

_____

_____

_____

_____

_____

What's your favorite Movie? Why?

_____

_____

_____

_____

_____

_____

If your life was a movie, would be an entertaining one?

_____

_____

_____

_____

_____

_____

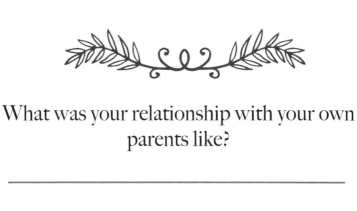

What was your relationship with your own parents like?

_____

_____

_____

_____

_____

Were your parents strict? Was your Mom or Dad the strictest?

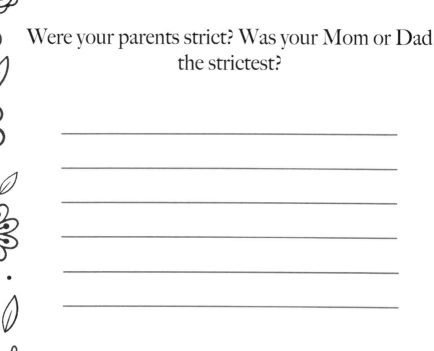

_____

_____

_____

_____

_____

Was there something your parents did when you were a kid that you swore you'd never do yourself?

_____

_____

_____

_____

_____

What's the most trouble you've ever gotten in?

_____

_____

_____

_____

_____

What's your favorite photo of yourself? Of our family?

Who was your first girlfriend/boyfriend?

_____

_____

_____

_____

_____

What were your exs like? How did you know they weren't «the One»?

_____

_____

_____

_____

_____

Place a picture and tell its story

How many serious relationships were you in before
you settled down? What were they like?

How many times were in love?

_____

_____

_____

_____

_____

What was your hardest breakup like?

_____

_____

_____

_____

_____

If you could plan out your perfect day, what would it entail? Tell me what you'd want to involve in it.

What was the most romantic thing dad did with you?

_____

_____

_____

_____

_____

_____

_____

_____

_____

_____

_____

_____

_____

_____

_____

_____

_____

Have you ever smoked pot before?

_____

_____

_____

_____

_____

Did you ever get arrested? If not, what did you do
that you should have been arrested for?

_____

_____

_____

_____

_____

What was your first car?

_____

_____

_____

_____

_____

What's your fondest memory in your first car?

_____

_____

_____

_____

_____

What are the 3 happiest times in your life?

_____

_____

_____

_____

_____

_____

_____

_____

_____

_____

_____

_____

_____

_____

_____

_____

What was the best gift I ever gave you?

_____

_____

_____

_____

_____

What's your favorite smell — perfume or otherwise?

_____

_____

_____

_____

_____

Who was the strangest person you've ever met?

_____
_____
_____
_____
_____

Who was your role model growing up? Did you
feel like you chose a good role model?

_____
_____
_____
_____
_____

Was there ever a serious mistake that you made that you regret to this day? How did you deal with it?

_____

_____

_____

_____

_____

_____

_____

_____

_____

_____

_____

_____

_____

_____

_____

_____

Who is someone you admire? Why?

_____

_____

_____

_____

_____

If you could have dinner with one person, dead or alive, who would it be?

_____

_____

_____

_____

_____

Do you have any health issues you've never told me about?

_____

_____

_____

_____

_____

What do I need to know about our family's medical history that could affect my health or life?

_____

_____

_____

_____

_____

What advice would you give to your younger self at age 20? 30? 40?

Is the present year anything like you imagined it would be when you were growing up?

_____

_____

_____

_____

_____

If you could change one thing about your life what would it be and why?

_____

_____

_____

_____

_____

What is one thing you know to be true?

_____

_____

_____

_____

_____

What do you think the greatest invention has been during your lifetime?

_____

_____

_____

_____

_____

What would your perfect day be like? Describe it.

_____

_____

_____

_____

_____

_____

_____

_____

_____

_____

_____

_____

_____

_____

_____

_____

_____

What do you want or wish most for your kids?

_____

_____

_____

_____

_____

_____

_____

_____

_____

_____

_____

_____

_____

What do you want your funeral to be like?

_____

_____

_____

_____

_____

_____

_____

_____

_____

_____

_____

_____

_____

_____

_____

_____

_____

_____